REAL
BiOS

PHARRELL

WILLIAMS

By Marie Morreale

Children's Press®
An Imprint of Scholastic Inc.
New York   Toronto   London   Auckland   Sydney
Mexico City   New Delhi   Hong Kong
Danbury, Connecticut

Library of Congress Cataloging-in-Publication Data
Morreale, Marie, author.
  Pharrell Williams / by Marie Morreale.
    pages cm. — (Real bios)
  Includes bibliographical references and index.
  ISBN 978-0-531-21378-0 (library binding) — ISBN 978-0-531-21431-2 (pbk.)
1. Williams, Pharrell—Juvenile literature. 2. Rap musicians—United States—Biography—Juvenile literature. I. Title.
  ML3930.W55M67 2015
  782.421649092—dc23 [B]   2014036212

Pharrell is everywhere— even at the 2014 Coachella Festival!

MEET PHARRELL!
FANTASTIC, FABULOUS & FUN!

Singer, rapper, **producer**, and songwriter Pharrell Williams may seem like an overnight success to some. But that isn't the case at all. This baby-faced star has been making music and magic for more than two decades! This *Real Bio* will take you through his amazing journey. Throughout his career, Pharrell has worked with many of music's biggest stars, including Justin Timberlake and Britney Spears. More recently, he has even added megastars such as One Direction, Ed Sheeran, and Ariana Grande to the list!

In these pages, you'll find silly stories, heartfelt memories, and outrageous info about Pharrell and his family and friends. Even more importantly, you'll see how much his fans mean to him.

Get ready to fly with Pharrell!

CONTENTS

Pharrell wows the audience at the Nickelodeon Kids' Choice Sports Awards 2014.

PROUD TO BE A
N.E.R.D.

FROM SKATEBOARD P TO PHARRELL

Pharrell Williams has always been a standout. But when he was born in Virginia Beach, Virginia, no one could have predicted that he would become the top music producer of the 2000s. Or that he would have number one hits as a solo artist. But that was his future.

Pharrell's parents, Pharaoh and Carolyn Williams, loved music. "Music's always been a part of my life," Pharrell told *Rolling Stone* magazine. "My grandmother used to play a lot of gospel, like the Mighty Clouds of Joy. My mom and dad played all that old [stuff]: Earth, Wind and Fire, Teddy Pendergrass, Michael Jackson, Stevie Wonder. I used to stare into the radio and visualize the music."

Words to Live By

"You have to be unafraid to dream."

Pharrell today and in his Princess Anne High School yearbook photo.

But as much as the Williams family loved to listen to music, none of them thought of it as a possible career. Pharaoh was a handyman, and Carolyn was an elementary school teacher.

"I never set out to do music," Pharrell explained to *CosmoGirl* magazine. "I didn't even think that was a *possibility*. I'm from Virginia—it's not New York, Los Angeles, or Chicago, where there is a music scene. In Virginia, there's no music. Nowhere to be found."

Yet somehow, somewhere, music was already inside Pharrell. "It was cool to drum on the tables at lunch," he continued with *CosmoGirl*. "On the bus on the way home, we'd recite the hottest songs that were out. It was developed there, but when you're young, you don't

Radio interview time! Pharrell chats it up at L.A.'s Power 106's Big Boys Neighborhood show.

"IN MY FORMATIVE YEARS MUSIC WAS REAL TO ME."

realize that's development. You just look at it like you're having fun."

Looking back now, Pharrell understands that it was more than just fun. It was his passion. "I think [music] was my environment," Pharrell said in an interview with Oprah Winfrey. He even made the talk show icon laugh when he recalled playing music on his grandmother's pots and pans. "I took her pillows

The Neptunes arrive! Pharrell and producing partner Chad Hugo stop for snaps at the 2004 BET Awards.

and I took her egg beater and the whisk, and I would make my little drum sets," he explained. "And she said to me, 'You know, you like the drums. I'm going to buy you a drum. I want you to learn,' and I was like 'okay.'"

By the time Pharrell was in middle school, there had been a lot of changes in the Williams's household. His middle brother, Cato, had been born. The family moved from an apartment in the city to the suburbs of Virginia Beach. Pharrell also started going to a new school. "I went to a magnet school for music and art that was a center for the gifted and talented," he told *CosmoGirl*. "It was where all of us slightly less academic-minded kids went. So music just really helped explain who I was as a person. It made it a little more clear."

Of course, Pharrell had help along the way—his music teachers. He still remembers them well. "I think my life changed because [band camp was] where I met my first band teacher, Mrs. Warren," he told Oprah. "She would say, 'You know, I'm trying to teach you this lesson and you keep making all these other drum noises. You need to pay more attention.' And so I did. Then I met my second music teacher, Mr. Warren [Mrs. Warren's husband]. Then I met my third music teacher, Mr. Edwards. He tapped me and kind of said, 'You know, you have something.'"

Mr. Sharps, Pharrell's last music teacher, agreed. He encouraged Pharrell to pursue his talent with drive and determination. Pharrell has never forgotten the lessons and encouragement he received from his teachers. "Well, what am I without them?" he told CBS News. "Just try that for a second. Take all of my band teachers out of this. Where am I? I'm back in Virginia, doing something completely different."

Another person played a major part in Pharrell's early

Life Motto
"Don't play the rules . . . play by the rules!"

story—his friend Chad Hugo. The boys met in band camp. Pharrell played the drums and sang, and Chad played the saxophone.

Though they went to different high schools, they kept in touch after camp ended. They even played in bands together at school talent shows and events. One of these bands was a four-piece R&B group they formed with two friends named Shay Haley and Mike Etheridge. They named themselves the Neptunes. Pharrell and Chad liked performing. However, they soon found that they were more interested in the recording studio **mixing board**. They were happy producing their own songs or ones performed by other artists.

When Pharrell wasn't in school or playing music, he did normal teenage things. He even worked at

McDonald's a couple of times. "I got fired—every time," he told *GQ* magazine. "I had good managers. I was just lazy."

He hit the local skate parks whenever he could. As a matter of fact, he was nicknamed Skateboard P—though he later confessed that he gave himself the nickname!

In other words, Pharrell was a typical teenager. He loved music, but he didn't understand just how talented he was. He got his first hint when R&B legend Teddy Riley opened up his Future Recording Studio. Many famous artists came to record

FACT FILE

THE BASICS

AME: Pharrell Williams

ROFESSIONAL NAME: Pharrell

NICKNAME: Skateboard P

BIRTHDAY: April 5, 1973

BIRTH SIGN: Aries

BIRTHPLACE: Virginia Beach, Virginia

CURRENT RESIDENCE: Miami, Florida

PARENTS: Pharaoh and Carolyn Williams

SIBLINGS: Two younger brothers, Cato and Psolomon; two half brothers, Pharaoh and David

WIFE: Helen Lasichanh

SON: Rocket Ayer Williams

HIGH SCHOOL: Princess Anne High School

IDOL: Scientist Carl Sagan

INSTRUMENTS: Drums, piano

TEEN FASHION STYLE: Stan Smith shoes, Vision Street Wear, T-shirts, plaid pants, trucker hats

Fashion Icon
Pharrell was voted the Best Dressed Man in the World by Esquire magazine in 2005.

at the studio, which was practically next door to Pharrell's school. "It was kind of like telling me that Jesus, E.T., and Elvis are going to walk in at any moment," Pharrell told *W* magazine. "It was incredible—just the biggest, luckiest thing that could have happened in my life."

Pharrell and Chad soon came to Riley's attention. One of Riley's employees saw them at a high school talent show and passed on word of their skills. By the time they graduated high school, Pharrell and Chad were producing far more than performing. They showed such promise

FAVORITES

"WHAT I LOVE ABOUT SPONGEBOB IS THAT HE'S BASICALLY A SIX-YEAR-OLD

PORT: Skateboarding

PLACE IN THE WORLD: Japan

FASHION STATEMENT: Unique hats and a comfortable T-shirt

DESIGNERS: Louis Vuitton, Lanvin, Ralph Lauren Purple Label, Comme des Garçons

SHOES: Adidas

SNACKS: Cherry Pop-Tarts, Rice Krispies Treats, crunchy cookie butter on Nilla Wafers

CEREALS: Cinnamon Toast Crunch, Corn Pops, Fruity Pebbles

FOOD: Japanese

MIAMI RESTAURANT: Pubbelly Sushi

NEW YORK/LOS ANGELES RESTAURANT: Nobu

ICE-CREAM TRUCK CHOICE: Banana Fudge Bomb Pop

FLOWERS: Daisies

GROCERY STORE: Trader Joe's

MOVIES: Gravity, Close Encounters of the Third Kind, Cloud Atlas

ACTOR: Bill Murray

BOOK: The Alchemist by Paulo Coelho

SOCIAL MEDIA: Vine

TV SHOWS/NETWORKS: The Discovery Channel, SpongeBob SquarePants, Adventure Time, and Boomerang

CARTOON CHARACTER: SpongeBob SquarePants

MUSICIANS: Michael Jackson, Stevie Wonder

PASTIME: Browsing in bookstores

that Teddy Riley hired them as a production team. Though they were no longer a band, they continued calling themselves the Neptunes.

Starting in 1992, the Neptunes wrote and produced songs for some of the biggest names in R&B, pop, and hip-hop. These superstars included Nelly, Jay Z, Diddy, Britney Spears, Justin Timberlake, and Snoop Dogg, among many others. By the end of the 1990s, the Neptunes were considered the premiere production team in music. In 2001, they produced Britney's "I'm a Slave 4 U," which was their first number one worldwide hit. However, as much as Pharrell loved the behind-the-scenes work, he still loved to perform. That's what led Pharrell and Chad to form a new band with their old friend Shay Haley. They called themselves N.E.R.D.

In 2003 the Neptunes released their *Clones* CD.

The band's first album, *In Search Of...*, was released in Europe in 2001 and in the United States the following year. It sold fairly well, but Pharrell and Chad were breaking more records as the Neptunes. In 2002, the Neptunes were named Producers of the Year at both the Billboard Music Awards and the Source Awards.

Chad and Pharrell enjoy meeting fans at an autograph signing for *Clones*.

The Neptunes were known for their ability to mix R&B, hip-hop, rap, pop, and rock to highlight the unique talents of all the artists they worked with. One article called them "the United Nations of pop." Pharrell explained to the *New York Daily News*, "You can't pinpoint what we do. Right when people think they know our direction, we take a left."

In 2003, a survey showed that the Neptunes had produced 43 percent of the songs played on the radio at that time. Some of these hits even featured Pharrell's singing and rapping. In 2004, N.E.R.D. released their second album, *Fly or Die*, and the Neptunes collected two Grammys for their work on Justin Timberlake's *Justified*. To cap off the year, the duo produced Snoop Dogg's classic song "Drop It Like It's Hot," which hit the top of *Billboard*'s charts.

With all his success as a producer, Pharrell found the desire to perform again. So, in 2006, he released his first album as a solo artist, *In My Mind*. Critics claimed it lacked Pharrell's usual magic touch. What happened?

After a lot of thought, Pharrell realized that he didn't really know himself. "I *thought* I knew who I was," he told *The Guardian*. "This competitive guy in the music industry, who admired

Pharrell accepts the Producer of the Year, Non-Classical, for the Neptunes at the 46th Annual Grammy Awards.

my peers and felt he needed to compete with the races that they designed. But in life you're meant to race against yourself."

Pharrell now says that the songs on *In My Mind* were about experiences and paths he had never taken. He was trying to use ideas that might have been good for Jay Z, Kanye West, or Snoop Dogg in his own songs. But it just wasn't him. "It was in my mind, but not my heart," he told *The Guardian*.

It took a lot of reflection for Pharrell to put things in place. Like the professional he truly is, Pharrell picked himself up and set new goals to conquer. He knew the direction he was going to take, and he was ready to take it on.

Friends and collaborators Jay Z and Pharrell celebrate yet another Grammy win!

Child's Play

"Tom and Jerry raised me. I was drawn to Looney Tunes, Disney, Pixar."

Pharrell introduces his Billionaire Boys Club apparel line and store in New York City.

PHARRELL THE ARTIST

PRODUCER . . . SONGWRITER . . . SOLO ARTIST . . . NUMBER ONE STAR!

The year 2006 was a turning point for Pharrell. He began to question where he was going professionally and personally. He told *GQ* that his life seemed to be "talking about the money I was making and the by-products of living that lifestyle. What was that about? What'd you get out of it? There was no purpose. I was so under the wrong impression at that time. . . . I wanted to be like Jay Z. I wanted to be like Puff. Those are their paths. I got my own path. But I didn't know what my path was. I knew that I was meant to do something different. I knew that I needed to inject purpose in my music. And I thought that was my path."

So how did Pharrell make that change? He got back to basics and relied on his talent and hard work. However, Pharrell's new journey included lots of side roads. He was known as a fierce producer, a music master who would work on a project nonstop until he got it right. Music had always been the center of his life. Those closest to him knew that there was an inner businessman in him, too. He was ready to make moves. He didn't need to re-create himself. He just wanted to expand himself and his "brand." And this new path was going to show just who Pharrell really was. "If you asked me my favorite brand, I'd say individuality," he told *USA Today*.

Fashion has always been an important expression for Pharrell. He wasn't interested in just buying designer wear. Though he might choose a Comme des Garçons jacket, it might be paired with regular old jeans. "I consider myself an ordinary person, and I get my style from everyday people," he told *USA Today* about his fashion sense.

Pharrell's Timeline

From Then 2 Now

1992
Pharrell and his friend Chad Hugo start their production team, the Neptunes

2001
Pharrell, Chad, and Shay Haley start the music group N.E.R.D.

Pharrell is also proud of his ICECREAM Footwear line.

Pharrell's unique personal style was there from the time he was a teen, and he definitely made it his own. It was natural for him to turn to the fashion world. He designed sunglasses for Marc Jacobs and jewelry for Louis Vuitton. He even started his own clothing labels, Billionaire Boys Club and ICECREAM.

Of course, the businessman Pharrell never lost sight of his main love—music. In recent years, he has worked

JULY 25, 2006
Pharrell's first album as a solo artist, *In My Mind*, is released

OCTOBER 16, 2012
Pharrell releases his first book, *Pharrell: Places and Spaces I've Been*

JULY 3, 2013
Despicable Me 2 opens, introducing the world to Pharrell's "Happy"

Pharrell and Gwen Stefani perform "Can I Have It Like That" at the American Music Awards.

with artists such as Kendrick Lamar, Gwen Stefani, Beyoncé, Shakira, Jennifer Lopez, and dozens more. In 2013, one of his biggest successes ever came from his lead vocals on Daft Punk's smash single "Get Lucky." The same year, he also lent his voice to two other huge hits—Robin Thicke's "Blurred Lines," which features Pharrell and rapper T.I., and "Happy," which Pharrell wrote for the movie *Despicable Me 2*.

While both songs were chart toppers, "Happy" became an utter **phenomenon**. The song was written for the

JANUARY 26, 2014
At the 56th Grammy Awards, Pharrell wins Producer of the Year, Non-Classical; Record of the Year and Best Pop Duo/Group Performance for Daft Punk's "Get Lucky"; and Album of the Year for Daft Punk's *Random Access Memories*

MARCH 2, 2014
At the 86th Academy Awards, Pharrell is nominated for Best Original Song for "Happy"

Despicable Me 2 character Gru. The movie's producers wanted a song that might touch Gru's cold, cold heart. Pharrell wrote a number of songs, but the producers turned them all down. "I was at zero," Pharrell told *W*. "After nine different songs, recorded fully, they were like, 'No, no, no, no.' So I went back and wrote 'Happy.' I didn't have the melody, just the chorus. For 20 minutes after I finished, I was jumping around the room. I told [the producer] to listen to the song in his car, that if he didn't like 'Happy,' I didn't know what to give him."

It worked! Everyone thought "Happy" was perfect for the movie. Surprisingly, radio stations weren't interested in the song at first. But Pharrell wasn't going to be stopped. He decided that "Happy" needed a visual. On November 21, 2013, Pharrell released a 24-hour-long interactive video of

Splish Splash
Pharrell often writes his songs when he's in the shower!

MARCH 3, 2014
Pharrell's second solo album, *G I R L*, is released

MARCH 20, 2014 The United Nations teams up with Pharrell to declare an International Day of Happiness

APRIL 5, 2014
Pharrell performs on *Saturday Night Live* for the first time, on his birthday

Pharrell and Daft Punk won Record of the Year for "Get Lucky" at the 56th Annual Grammy Awards.

"Happy." It was called, "24 Hours of Happy." Special guests such as Jimmy Kimmel, Magic Johnson, Steve Carell, Jamie Foxx, Miranda Cosgrove, and Janelle Monáe made appearances. Everyone in the video danced to the catchy, upbeat song.

The music video began showing up everywhere, turning the song into a huge hit. It was played on radio and TV and downloaded by countless people. "Happy"

APRIL 24, 2014
Pharrell announces *Inspiration*, an interactive digital book that will be co-written by fans online

MAY 2014
Pharrell remixes "Last Night, Good Night" for artist Takashi Murakami's movie *Jellyfish Eyes*

MAY 2, 2014
The Amazing Spider-Man 2 opens—Pharrell worked on the movie score with composer and producer Hans Zimmer

and "Blurred Lines" earned Pharrell seven Grammy Award nominations in 2014.

Pharrell believes that life is a big circle, and he proved it to himself in 2014. After his success in 2013, Columbia Records approached him about making another solo album. After some persuasion, Pharrell realized he was in a better place than he had been during the making of *In My Mind*. It might be the right time to go it alone again. On March 3, 2014, he released *G I R L*, his second album as a solo artist.

"I instantly knew that the name of the album was called *G I R L*, and the reason why is because women and girls,

Jennifer Lopez helped Pharrell celebrate winning the 2014 iHeartRadio Music Innovator Award.

SEPTEMBER 2, 2014
Cara Delevingne presents Pharrell the 2014 British GQ Award for Best Solo Artist

SEPTEMBER 5, 2014
Pharrell's G I R L fragrance hits shelves in the United States

SEPTEMBER 9, 2014
Pharrell starts the European leg of his Dear Girl tour in Manchester, England

SEPTEMBER 22, 2014
Pharrell debuts as a new judge on NBC's *The Voice*

The cast of Season 7 of *The Voice*: (l-r) Adam Levine, Carson Daly, Gwen Stefani, Blake Shelton, and Pharrell.

for the most part, have just been so loyal to me and supported me," he told *GQ*.

Even though Pharrell's schedule was already jam-packed, he decided to fill in the blanks. Along with old friend Gwen Stefani, Pharrell joined the cast of the hit NBC music series *The Voice*. Why would Pharrell add a summer of taping **auditions** to his must-do list? Simple—he loves discovering new talent.

"Producing is what I do every day, talking to people about what they want in their track, giving them advice about what sounds good **juxtaposed** with their voice and their style," he told the *Wall Street Journal*. "That's what I'll be doing on the show, but it's a huge platform, and

"I'M PROUD OF ALL MY WORK AND I'M THANKFUL. BUT 'HAPPY' CHANGED ME."

it's about paying it forward. The universe has been good to me, so it's like, 'What can I share with you guys?' I'm hoping that some person in Iowa can take some of my advice, internalize it and go and be bigger than all of us put together."

Pharrell loves being a part of something—whether it's a band, a business, a project, a charity, or, most importantly, his family. He is married to model and designer Helen Lasichanh, and they have a young son named Rocket Williams. When Pharrell first met Helen at an industry event, something clicked instantly. "She just reminded me so much of myself, like [she's] different, marches to the beat of her own drum," he told Oprah. "And she just stood out. And I was like, 'Who and what is

Pharrell loves finding new talent, so *The Voice* is perfect for him.

that?' I just knew . . . I was just enamored by the moment I was having with her. I just wanted to read that book."

When the couple had their son in 2008, he rounded out the family—they were a complete circle. Of course, everyone wondered why they named him Rocket! Well, Oprah asked! Pharrell explained to her, "Because in the same way . . . the Indians name their children like . . . a force or an animal or an element, we named him after a man-made machine that was meant to . . . ascend."

"WHEN I WAS YOUNG, I THOUGHT I KNEW EVERYTHING."

Pharrell says he and wife Helen Lasichanh are "best friends."

Helen holds her and Pharrell's son, Rocket. Such a cutie!

Success, happiness, and direction—these are the things Pharrell and his family seek. Though any door in the world would open for them, they aren't often seen at glitzy, glamorous events.

"We appreciate our privacy, but at the end of the day we are normal people," he told Oprah. "When I'm not working, we are homebodies and Helen's my best friend. We spend more time jumping on the bed than we do partying, clinking glasses."

When Oprah followed up and asked how he remained so normal, so undistracted by fame and fortune, Pharrell simply said, "I know that none of this is my doing. I know I'm just a puzzle piece in this big mosaic that the universe conspired to happen, and I'm happy being that little comma in the sentence."

Pharrell is one of the most loved and respected members of the music industry.

PHARRELL OPENS UP

SCHOOL DAYS, CELEBRITY BFFS, BEING FAMOUS, & MORE!

Though he is a megamaster of music, Pharrell isn't afraid to reveal just what a normal guy he is when a reporter or even a fan interviews him. And he will talk about anything—his school days, running from bears, and his big fuzzy, yellow Mickey Mouse slippers. Read all about it!

On the hardest-working artists he has produced . . . "The ones who are really successful work really hard. Beyoncé works hard. I appreciate that. Justin [Timberlake], Usher, and Jay Z work hard. They're not in the studio to [mess] around. We all have fun, but when it's time for us to put our Jedi hats on, we put on our Jedi hats and battle it out with the creativity that exists in oblivion. We reach in and snatch it out and carve away until it's right."

On enjoying your school years . . . "Go to dances, perform in talent shows, all of that. . . . I played [drums] in the school band from seventh grade on. I cherish all the time I spent in high school. It all goes by so fast, and you never get to do that stuff over again."

On the party scene . . . "I'm done with parties. I do more reading and things like that. I like getting all the information I can get. I'm a Discovery Channel junkie! When you're at a party, you're giving away a lot of energy. I'd rather be consuming great energy."

Pharrell is also a style icon.

On the big, fuzzy, yellow slippers he always wears in the studio and at home . . . "They're Mickey [Mouse]'s feet slippers from Disney World. They were given to me by a friend. But I go to Disney World maybe twice a year, and every time I go I buy all the pairs they

Pharrell has fans of all ages! The kids help bring out his inner child.

have. In one of my closets, I have, like, a dozen pairs of Mickey slippers. They're so comfortable."

On if he has ever gone camping . . . "Never. I'm not into running from bears."

On how he feels about his fans . . . "I took a lot of years to understand the value of things and the value of the people you work with. The value of your fans who ultimately hold you high and lift you up. We're just hang gliders, dude, and they are carrying us around."

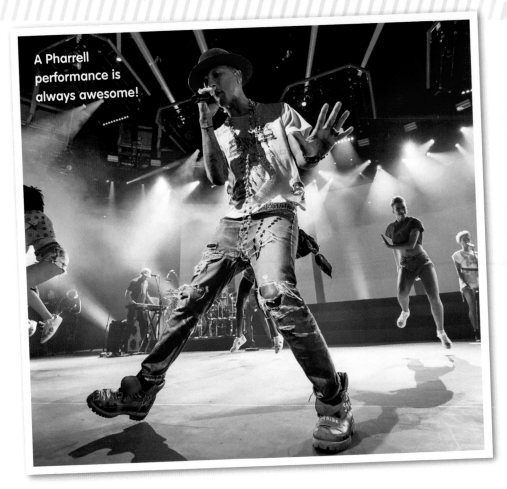

A Pharrell performance is always awesome!

On how he feels when he sees people wearing his Billionaire Boys Club clothes . . .

"It's really amazing when I see kids wearing the label at my shows or on the streets. It never gets old."

On breaking into the fashion industry . . .

"Study the greats."

On keeping in shape . . .

"People look back at the 'Beautiful' video, and I had love handles, man. I had to get rid of them. So I'm up to 675 sit-ups every morning. Also, cut down on bread . . . You do 300 sit-ups and take a shower, man, you're going to have an incredible day."

On something he isn't good at . . . "Basketball. I learned how to shoot a mean free throw, but my game [is the worst]. I challenge myself: If there's something I'm not good at, I'm gonna work at it."

On the best part of being famous

. . . "The part that means the most is the music, which is the same thing that moved me when I was dead broke. It's the same thing that moved me as a child—being six years old and sitting in the back of my grandmother's Datsun, listening to Earth, Wind & Fire's chord changes and looking at the stars."

How many different hats do you think Pharrell has?

FUN WITH PHARRELL!

LISTS . . . FACTS . . . QUOTES GALORE!

McPHARRELL

Pharrell produced the "I'm Lovin' It" commercial jingle for McDonald's.

FIRSTS

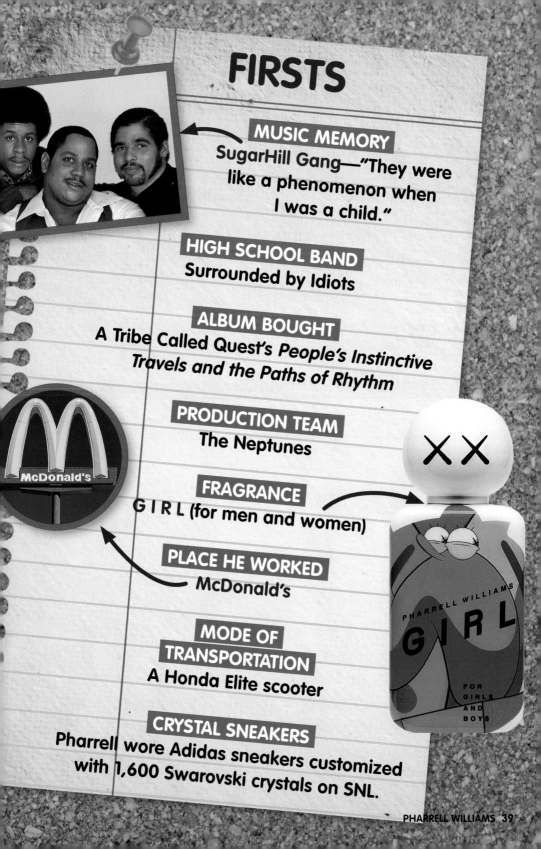

MUSIC MEMORY
SugarHill Gang—"They were like a phenomenon when I was a child."

HIGH SCHOOL BAND
Surrounded by Idiots

ALBUM BOUGHT
A Tribe Called Quest's *People's Instinctive Travels and the Paths of Rhythm*

PRODUCTION TEAM
The Neptunes

FRAGRANCE
G I R L (for men and women)

PLACE HE WORKED
McDonald's

MODE OF TRANSPORTATION
A Honda Elite scooter

CRYSTAL SNEAKERS
Pharrell wore Adidas sneakers customized with 1,600 Swarovski crystals on SNL.

PHARRELL WILLIAMS, GIRL

FOR GIRLS AND BOYS

PHARRELL'S BFFS TALK

Justin Timberlake:
"When I decided to work on my first solo album in 2002, Pharrell was the first musician I spoke to. . . . I will never forget how free and fun those sessions were. . . . He made me fearless."

Ed Sheeran:
"[Pharrell] is a lovely, lovely man. Everything that comes out of his mouth is so warm and soulful. He's just a good human being. He's going to be a page in a history book, that's the way I could sum him up."

Mary J. Blige:
"Pharrell is a very sweet guy. If he writes a song, he writes the song for *you*."

Usher:
"We want to create music like you never heard before. Once we create something in the studio that everybody is crazy about, then we try to beat that. . . . We're challenging ourselves in the moment."

PHARRELL TALKS BACK ...

Beyoncé

"You set women free," he declares. "I'm trying to tell you, that [album, *Beyoncé,*] is a phenomenon."

Liam Payne

"Liam stopped by my studio. I think he's just genuinely curious about music. We have that in common. He's always wanting to see what's new and what's next."

Gwen Stefani

"She's my kind of girl. When it comes to Gwen, it's not fake, it's real; and if you don't like it, she's cool with it."

Lorde

"She's 16 years old. She is a shining example of where we are headed. . . . A 16-year-old who wrote her own song and was speaking about society. She's today's definition of a singer/songwriter."

THE HAT

No one has to explain themselves when they mention "Pharrell's Hat." Immediately, the image of Pharrell wearing his big hat at the 2014 Grammys comes to mind. Here are a few fun facts about that fabulous headgear!

HAT STAT

Pharrell's oversized hat has its own Twitter account—@pharrellhat.

ICONIC

The hat was displayed at the Newseum in Washington, D.C., for several months in 2014.

EBAY SALE

The hat was bought by the restaurant chain Arby's for $44,100. All the money went to Pharrell's charity From One Hand to AnOTHER.

HISTORY

Pharrell bought the hat in a store in West End, London. It is an original Vivienne Westwood, a 1970s designer to the stars.

OOPS MOMENTS

HAIRCUT HORROR
"When I was 11 and Mr. T was [popular], I got a Mohawk. My dad cut it for me. Going to school with that haircut taught me a lot of humility."

SCHOOL DAZE
"I would put Cheerios in my ice cream. At school, I used to do the Robot down the hall every day. I wasn't a nerd, just . . . different."

MIDNIGHT HOUR
"I'd work in the studio after school and wouldn't tell [my parents] about it. . . . My curfew was midnight, and I used to get into trouble for coming in late."

PRANK CALL
Pharrell was in the studio once and he got two phone calls from someone who said he was Michael Jackson. Pharrell hung up, thinking it was a joke. On the third call, his manager urged him to talk . . . it was really Michael Jackson. "So I picked up the phone and he's like 'Hello . . . It's Michael [crunch, crunch].' He was eating popcorn in my ear. . . . I knew it was him."

Before *The Voice*'s Season 7 was over, Pharrell was asked to come back for Season 8!

PHARRELL...
DOWN THE LINE
ALWAYS READY TO LEARN SOMETHING NEW!

"'m somebody who takes advantage of the present moment," Pharrell told *USA Today*. "It's the only thing in this world where you can turn nothing into something."

Pharrell has always known that success and happiness aren't just handed to you. They are things you have to work for. But first you have to determine what path you want to take.

"I think we're all dealt these cards in life, but the cards in and of themselves don't read one way or the other," he told *Interview.* "It's up to you to home in and cultivate whatever you've got in your hand. I make my decisions based on my gut—and I don't always make the right ones."

> **"I HAVE AN APPRECIATIVE NATURE. I USUALLY GO TO SLEEP SMILING."**

But even then, Pharrell picks up the cards and deals a new hand. What he is looking for are ways to express his talents and encourage people, especially kids, to do the same. That is one reason why he started the foundation From One Hand to AnOTHER. Its mission is to "change the world one kid at a time by providing them the tools and resources to meet their unique potential." This is something Pharrell will be working on for years to come.

As for his music, the future will include producing and songwriting, especially for new artists. Yet, if something interesting comes along, don't be surprised if he goes in a new direction. But he knows his priorities. "Music will always be my first love," he told *W.* "But the one thing I've learned is that this life is a movie and I am co-creator. It's a big movie and there's a lot of creativity going on. As long as I play my part, it won't be over for quite a while."

Lesson 2
Learn
"How to slow down."

Resources

BOOK
Terrell Brown. *Pharrell Williams*. Broomall, PA: Mason Crest Publishers, 2007.

SHEET MUSIC
Pharrell Williams. "Happy (from *Despicable Me 2*)." Milwaukee, WI: Hal Leonard Corporation, 2013.

ARTICLE
The Red Bulletin, July 2014
   "Pharrell Williams Predicts the Future"

Visit this Scholastic Web site for more information on **Pharrell Willic**
www.factsfornow.scholastic.com
Enter the keywords **Pharrell Willian**

Glossary

auditions *(aw-DISH-uhnz)* short performances by actors, singers, musicians, or dancers to see whether they are suitable for a part in a play, concert, or other performance

juxtaposed *(JUHK-stuh-pohzd)* set side by side to show differences

mixing board *(MIK-sing BORD)* equipment used to control the volume and effects of individual parts of a recording

phenomenon *(fuh-NAH-muh-nahn)* something very unusual and remarkable

producer *(pruh-DOOS-ur)* a person who oversees the recording of a piece of a song or album

Index

Acknowledgments

Page 6: Music: *Rolling Stone* December 1, 2005
Page 8: Early music: *CosmoGirl* March 2004; Formative years: *Oprah Prime* April 13, 2014
Page 9: Drum Set: *Oprah Prime* April 13, 2014; Magnet school: *CosmoGirl* March 2014
Page 10: Teachers: *Oprah Prime* April 13, 2014; Life Motto: *TeenVogue* November 2010
Page 12: Working at McDonald's: *GQ* 2014
Page 14: Teddy Riley Studio: *W* May 7, 2014; SpongeBob: *TeenVogue*
Page 17: Neptunes: *NY Daily News* March 3, 2002
Page 18: Who he was: *The Guardian* March 7, 2014
Page 19: In his mind: *The Guardian* March 7, 2014; Child's Play: *USA Today* February 20, 2014
Page 21: His path: *GQ* March 2014

Page 22: Individuality: *USA Today* February 20, 2014; Everyday person: *USA Today* February 20, 2014
Page 25: Writing "Happy": *W* May 7, 2014
Page 27: *G I R L*: *GQ Style* April 2014
Page 28: *The Voice*: *Wall Street Journal*; Proud of his work: CBS News April 13, 2014
Page 29: Helen Lasichanh: *Oprah Prime* April 13, 2014
Page 30: Rocket: *Oprah Prime* April 13, 2014; When he was young: *W* May 7, 2014
Page 31: Privacy: *Oprah Prime* April 13, 2014
Page 33: Hardest working artist: *Rolling Stone* December 1, 2005
Page 34: School years: *TeenPeople* February 2004; Party scene: *Rolling Stone* December 1, 2005; Mickey Mouse slippers: *CosmoGirl*

August 2006
Page 35: Camping: *OK!* magazine
Page 36: BBC label: *TeenVogue* November 2010; Fashion industry: *TeenVogue* November 2010; Keeping in shape: *Blender* April 25, 2004
Page 37: Basketball: *Blender* April 25, 2004; Famous: *Spin* December 2005
Page 40: Justin Timberlake: *Time* April 23, 2014; Ed Sheeran: Capitalfm.com May 24, 2014; Mary J. Blige: *People* October 13, 2003; Usher: MTV News January 22, 2009
Page 41: Beyoncé: Rap-up.com January 4, 2014; Liam Payne: PopCrush.com June 23, 2014; Gwen Stefani: *Spin* December 2005; Lorde: Capitalxtra.com February 3, 2014

Page 43: Haircut: *Blender*; School daze: *Blender*; Midnight hour: *TeenPeople* February 2004; Prank call: *Jimmy Kimmell Live* May 7, 2014
Page 44: Present moment: *USA Today* February 20, 2014; Dealt cards: *Interview* magazine May 27, 2009
Page 45: Music/first love: *W* May 7, 2014; Appreciative nature: *USA Today* February 20, 2014

About the Author

Marie Morreale is the author of many official and unofficial celebrity biographies. She attended New York University as an English/creative writing major and began her writing and editorial career in New York City. As the editor of teen/music magazines *Teen Machine* and *Jam!*, she covered TV, film, and music personalities and interviewed superstars such as Michael Jackson, Britney Spears, and Justin Timberlake/*NSYNC. Morreale was also an editor/writer at Little Golden Books.

Today, she is the executive editor, Media, of Scholastic Classroom Magazines writing about pop-culture, sports, news, and special events. Morreale lives in New York City and is entertained daily by her two Maine coon cats, Cher and Sullivan.

W9-BNV-131

Fill in each blank with the letter that comes next in **ABC order**.

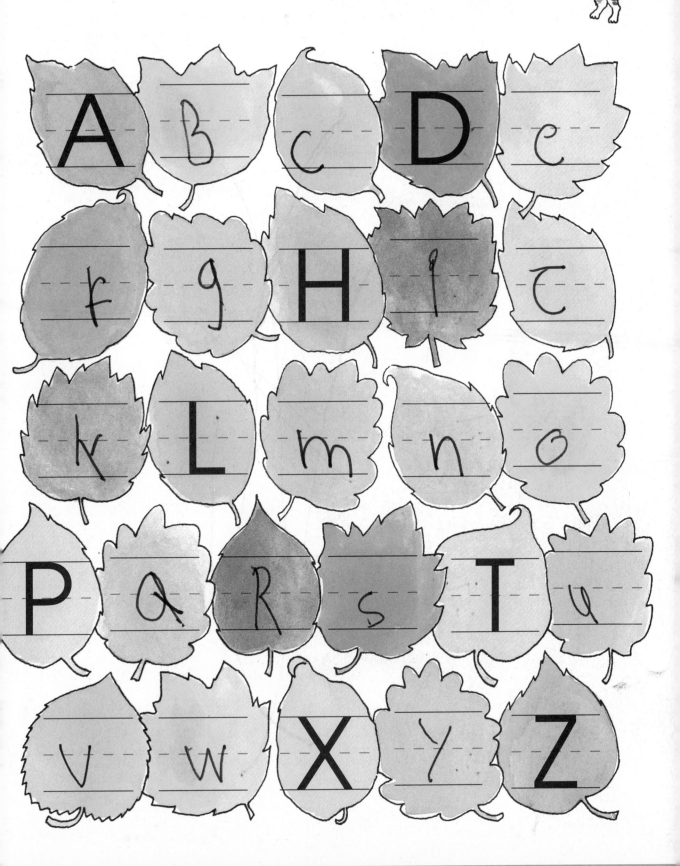

A B c D c

f g H i C

k L m n o

P Q R s T u

V w X y Z

Letter Match

Draw a line from each **uppercase** letter to the
lowercase letter that matches.

What Order?

Write each set of letters in **ABC order**.

F E D

Def

P O Q

T S R

M L N

Say the name of each picture.
Write **t** or **n** to begin the word.
Then write the word on the line.

___op

__tent

__nest

__nut

Say the name of each picture.
Write **m** or **p** to begin the word.
Then write the word on the line.

m oon

p ig

_____

- - - - - - - - - - - -

_____

_____

- - - - - - - - - - - -

_____

m an

p an

_____

- - - - - - - - - - - -

_____

_____

- - - - - - - - - - - -

_____

Say the name of each picture.
Write **d** or **t** to end the word.
Then write the word on the line.

be____

goa____

ca____

bir____

Say the name of each picture.
Write **m** or **n** to end the word.
Then write the word on the line.

su___

_____

- - - - - - - - - - -

_____

gu___

_____

- - - - - - - - - - -

_____

dru___

_____

- - - - - - - - - - -

_____

fa___

_____

- - - - - - - - - - -

_____

First, Next, Last

Write **1** in the square to show what happened **first**.
Write **2** to show what happened **next**.
Write **3** to show what happened **last**.

First, Next, Last

Write **1** in the square to show what happened **first**.
Write **2** to show what happened **next**.
Write **3** to show what happened **last**.

Which Two Go Together?

Draw a line from each **little** picture to the correct **big** picture.

Which Two Go Together?

In each row, circle the names of the pictures that **go together**.

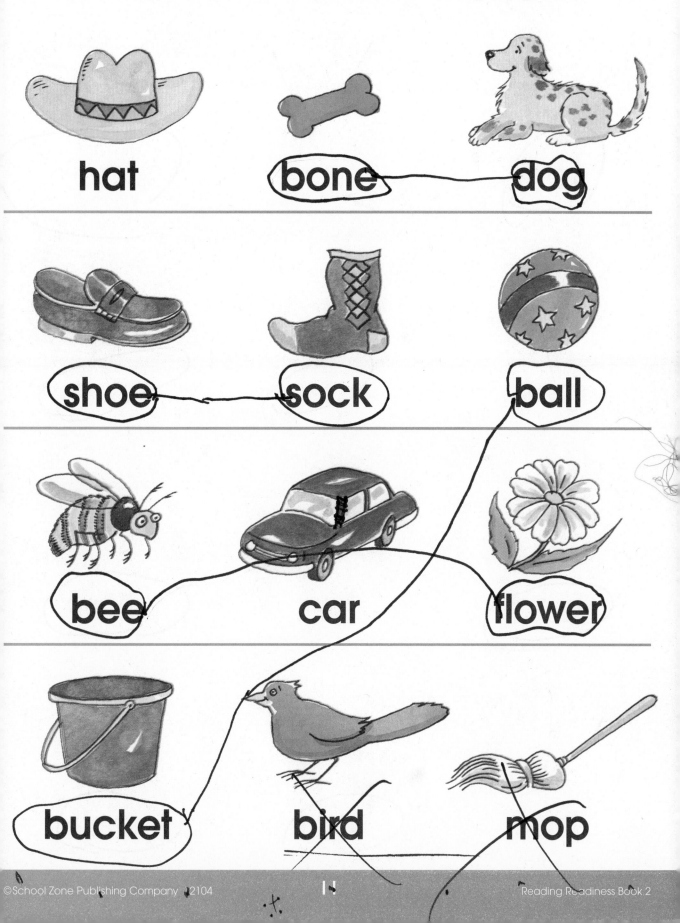

hat   bone   dog

shoe   sock   ball

bee   car   flower

bucket   bird   mop

Does Not Belong

In each row, circle the name of the picture that **does not belong**.

fork · fox · spoon

tree · horn · drum

bed · fan · pillow

box · bat · ball

Does Not Belong

In each row, circle the name of the picture that **does not belong**.

goat   pig   king

fish   house   barn

apple   bird   orange

hat   coat   cow

Color **two** ⭐ yellow.

Color **two** 🪐 yellow.

Color **two**  yellow.

Color **two** 👽 yellow.

Number Words

Draw a ◯ around the set of **7**.

Draw a ☐ around the set of **6**.

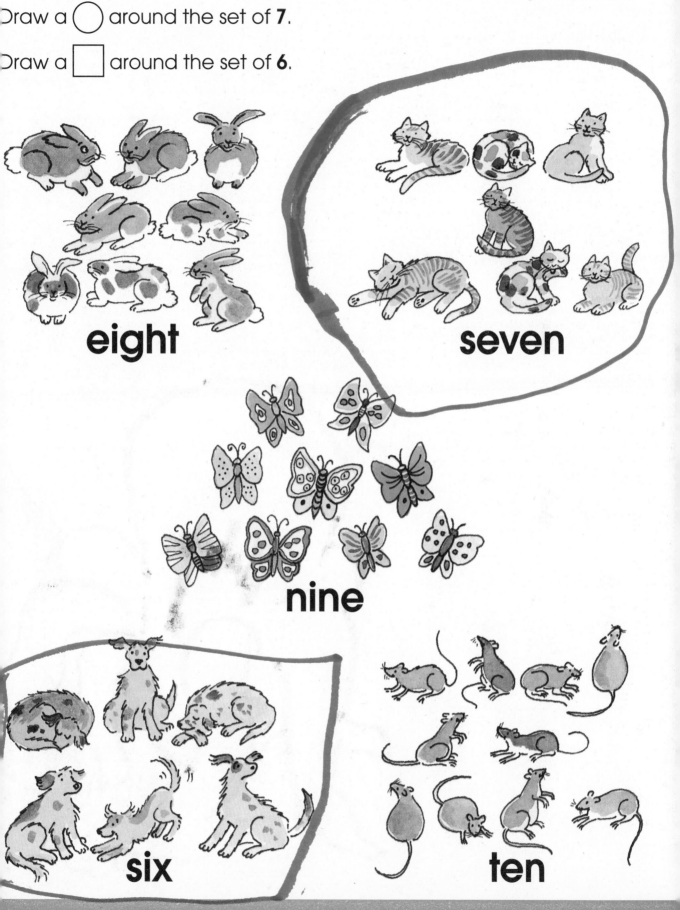

eight

seven

nine

six

ten

Color the Picture

Color the 🌿 green.

Color the 🪨 yellow.

Color the 🐟 blue.

Color the 🐙 purple.

Color the 👨‍🚀 orange.

Color the 📦 brown.

Color the ⛵ red.

Color the ⚓ black.

Color the ☁️ white.

Words that Rhyme

Draw a ◯ around each word that **rhymes** with **sing**.

Draw a ▢ around each word that **rhymes** with **ran**.

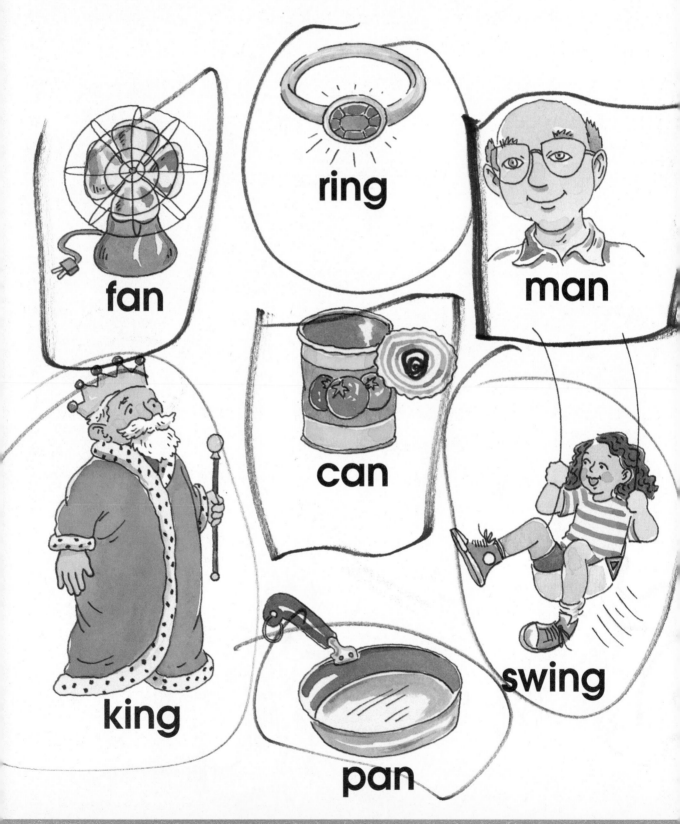

fan

ring

man

can

king

pan

swing

Words that Rhyme

Draw a ◯ around each word that **rhymes** with **sat**.

Draw a ▢ around each word that **rhymes** with **lake**.

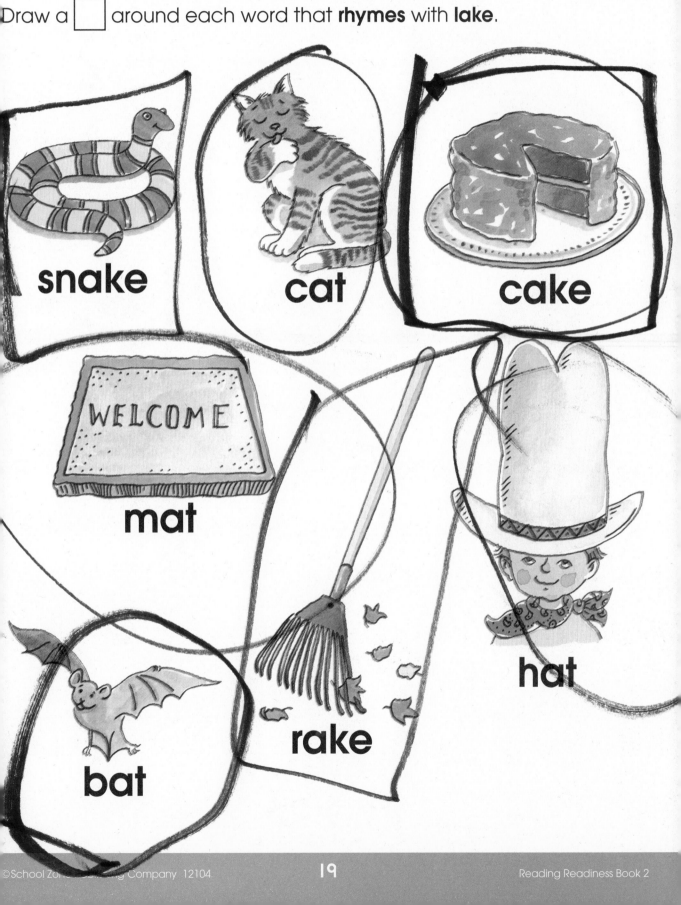

snake

cat

cake

mat

bat

rake

hat

Which is It?

Write the names of the **animals** on the **left**.
Write the names of the **plants** on the **right**.

dog

fish

flower

bush

tree

cow

animals

plants

Where Does It Belong?

Draw lines from the **foods** to the .

Draw lines from the **toys** to the .

apple

berry

doll

jacks

ball

cake

Draw a line from each word to the picture it names.

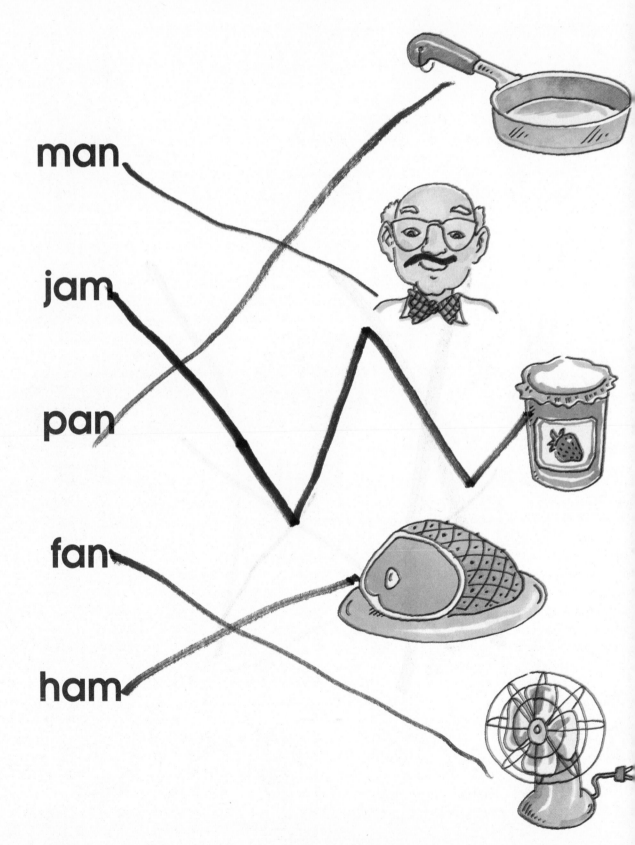

man

jam

pan

fan

ham

Draw a line from each word to the picture it names.

hen

goat

men

boat

pen

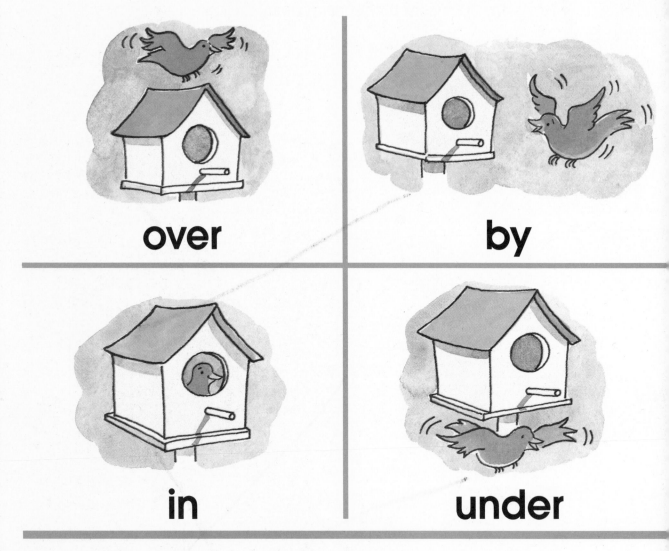

over

by

in

under

Write the word that tells **where** the bird is.

The bird is _____ the 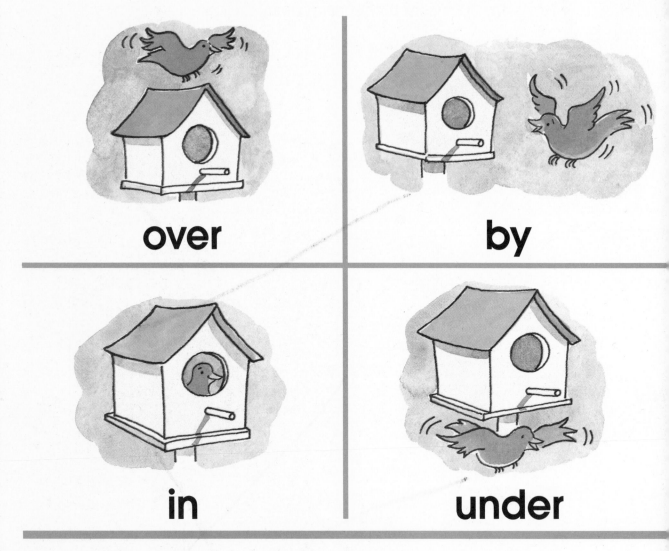 .

Write the word that tells **where** the bird is.

_____
_ _ _ _ _ _ _ _ _ _

The bird is _____ the  .

The bird is _____ the .

The bird is _____ the  .

Where is it?

on   **by**   **under**

Draw a red 🍎 **under** the 🪑 .

Draw a green 🍏 **on** the 🪑 .

Draw a yellow 🍏 **by** the 🪑 .

Write the correct **number** on each line.

How many  are **under** the ? _____

How many  are **in** the ? _____

How many  are **on** the ? _____

a b c d e f g h i j k l m n o p q r s t u v w x y z

cat **bat** **egg** **dog** **apple**

Write the words in **ABC order**.

apple

a b c d e f g h i j k l m n o p q r s t u v w x y z

elf   **fox**   **duck**   **goat**   **car**

Write the words in **ABC order**.

car

Underline the sentence that **goes with** each picture.

See the ball.

See the dog.

See the doll.

See the ball.

See the boat.

See the dog.

See the doll.

See the boat.

Underline the sentences that tell what you see.

There are two cows.

There are four balls.

There is a house.

There is one goat.

There is a girl.

AWARD

First Name:

Last Name:

has completed Reading Readiness, Book 2
from School Zone Publishing Company.